What to Keep

poems by

Carlene M. Gadapee

Finishing Line Press
Georgetown, Kentucky

What to Keep

ACKNOWLEDGMENTS

These poems have appeared in journals, some in slightly different forms:

"Valentine's Day" and "Re-twining" in *Smoky Quartz*
"Pandemic Easter, 2020" in *Global Poemic* as "Easter, 2020"
"1972" in *The Wild Word*
"1984," "Nana Cleans Out Her Desk," and "Sacred Heart" as "Yet If I Picture the Face of Jesus" in *The Henniker Review*
"Tissue Kisses" in *Think*
"Inheritance" in *The Blue Nib* as "Gifts"
"Border Children" in *Backchannels* as "Border Children: My Seventy-Seven-Year-Old Father Sits in His Rocking Chair and Weeps"
"Dry Weight, Twenty-one Grams, More or Less" in *Gyroscope Review*
"Breathing Exercises" in *Waterwheel*
"That Friday" in *Sojourn*
"Solving for X in a Pandemic" in *Streetlight Magazine*
"My Father's Hands" in *Inkwell*
"Free" in *Retrograde Review*

Publisher: Leah Huete de Maines
Editor: Christen Kincaid
Cover Art: Meghan K. Christ
Author Photo: Carlene M. Gadapee
Cover Design: Elizabeth Maines McCleavy

Order online: www.finishinglinepress.com
also available on amazon.com

Author inquiries and mail orders:
Finishing Line Press
PO Box 1626
Georgetown, Kentucky 40324
USA

Contents

In memory of my father, who read me all the stories and did all the voices, and with deep appreciation to my poet-teacher friends who helped me learn how to tell my own stories.

Finally, love and gratitude to Geoff and Meg.
Thank you for believing I could.

The Last Time

How do you know when something you do
will be the last time you do it? I mean, cook
the last meal, bring in the mail, clean counters,
lock the door? Sweep and mop the floor?

When you walk through empty rooms, scouting
for things you might have missed, what do you
look for? And if you don't find them, and you can't
go back, will you miss whatever they are? Or

when chores are done, and shades pulled down,
do you dust off your hands and turn away?
Can you say your good-byes too many times?
When it's the last time, and you know it, what can you say?

Valentine's Day

Here we are, and it's time to change
the calendar again, find a new month,
squared off and waiting. Do I buy you
a box of handkerchiefs or a Bruins jersey?
Should love be practical, or should it blow
the budget, buy the present that reminds us
what our hopes looked like. Correction:

look like. Hope gives us a square
to aim for, days away, to check off.
We will find ourselves squaring off
and looking forward yet again.

Pandemic Easter, 2020

Rough from so many ritualistic washings, twenty seconds each time,
                  "I will wash my hands in innocency,
                  so will I compass thine altar, O Lord…"
my ripping, winter-soft hands grasp and claw at dead things,
intent on scratching some small space for beauty. Brittle leaves,
                  "Take off the grave clothes…"
splintered grass, wind-blown paper and snow-faded candy wrappers
give way. Shifting raised forms into position feels like faith.
I find daffodils.

Re-twining

Who is this man who sits at the table?
What do we talk about? The tick
of the clock is loud, but never louder
than when children move out. Years
of being parents but not always partners
make it hard to untangle and re-twine
our lives. It's a careful negotiation:
untended growth needs to be retrained,
tied up, and given space to reach.
Our roots run deep.

1972

The rising hiss of cars shushes me, mid-imagining,
and the plashy drippings of an early morning rain
on wet pavement remind me that the past is mostly

fiction. Memories are imperfectly stitched together
with a yearning that hurts and cannot be helped.
White rose petals fall to the insistent rain. Maybe

I can almost capture a snug little wind-ward house
by a cove, a cascade of beach roses by graying posts
of a crooked fence tipped to the shifting sands.

Morning glory vines tangle with abandoned lobster
traps and curl around sea-worn rocks. Hidden tide-
pools shimmer in shadows. I'm looking for minnows

with Nana, a pint glass canning jar in my hand,
scooping a temporary playmate to watch until sunset.

She and I will wander back to the beach, content.
I release my wiggling captive to the waves.

Nana Cleans Out Her Desk

For a child, there was treasure to be found there:
pens and pencils, paperclips, old metal curlers, elastic
bands. Tiny pearl buttons rattled in the center drawer
alongside dark wheat pennies and brass fasteners.

The only drawer off limits was the bottom one, stuffed
with old bills, punched time cards, a few letters,
and flimsy air mail envelopes, ones used for overseas.

Nana sorted papers sitting on the worn rug, stacking piles.
She checked razored-open envelopes, one by one, each
as empty as the last. She was looking for *Support money.*
Just in case. She might have missed some. I didn't know
what abandoned meant, I didn't know about *divorce.*
When I think of loss, it looks like empty envelopes.

Ten

I am ten. I am always ten.
I do not yet have breasts.
I have not bled. I hold a ripe
tomato in my hand, warm
flesh, round, sweet and juicy,
not cut, just perfect. I am
smiling. My loose braids
are sun-bleached, my skin tan
and my eyes clear. I am ten.
I am smiling at the camera.
The tomato is yet uncut.

Sacred Heart

I know it to be false—this image—Godhead
with flowing blond locks—
sad blue eyes, searching.

The face should be of a man I know is Semitic.
I look around,
no one else seems troubled.

It's not at all like the wan, somber, bearded face
of someone who is deeply disappointed, or
pained by a loss
I didn't cause. This face makes little sense.
It's not historic, but
it's the one I grew up with, framed,
burning heart
looking like it might burst. That open heart
surrounded by flames scared me.

When I first heard the phrase heartburn
all I could think of was this picture on the wall,
electric blood glowing.

I wonder aloud: what do you see in me?
There's a silence,
a long pause. My own burning heart—
is it sacred too?

Tissue Kisses

Murmurs of muted brown, shades of cherry red,
a shell-pink gloss. Silver-dust tissue kisses
pile one on another in a cheap wicker basket.
Blotted rumors quickly hushed and discarded.

Strident drug-store tubes tested and smudged.
Small peach fans make surprise sunsets, open-
mouthed and wide. Crumpled poppies
and faded prom-corsage orchids wilt, crushed

and smeared. Creased, blowsy petals are
folded and pressed, scraps of flimsy origami
smile-ghosts. Wordless, forgotten, half-recalled:
transparent, triumphant, teen-aged wiles filter

echoes of plans made, exotic places to go—
shimmering promises of exes and ohs.

1984

I didn't tumble down the stairs, my wrist caught in the grasp
of a boy-man I'd just met. *Get to know you a little, let's get out
of this crowd* seemed reasonable. Inexperienced, a little more
than a little drunk, too easily led. I remember a muddy parking lot,
sheets of rain, oily grit in my hair. Blurry streetlamps weakly
illuminated the bumpers of the cars, rusty rocker panels,
my friends' reaching hands. *Are you okay? Here, eat this.*
Give you something to throw up. I didn't throw up.
Self-disgust doesn't come up that easily.
(*My fault?*)
Did I know how I got there? Yes, a car-load of us went.
Did I know where I was? No, I didn't drive and
it was dark. Do I remember the date? The guy's name? No.
Did I ever see him again, anywhere? Everywhere, nowhere.
No. I don't remember, sorry, I don't remember. I remember
the gravel, and which was rain and which was tears.

Words Cannot Be the Things We Want Them to Be

After Zbigniew Herbert

a warm house filled with hundreds of books
a kitchen with clean counters and cooling sourdough loaves
a back yard bordered by fruit trees surrounding expanses
of clover, dandelion, daisies, and purslane

a bookcase with creaking casters, scuffed and scratched,
volumes of poetry, crystal vases and glass inkwells,
feathered fans and teacups, a tin box of crayons
one signed baseball—never mind by whom,
it's unimportant—

a snug bedroom hung with watercolor paintings
framed photos, a small crucifix wound with a tangled scapular
a window facing a wooded hillside and horses, shaded
by half-closed blinds and grey dawn-light
one small pine dresser with worn pulls

> I only name the things that remind me of who I am
> a quiet life,
> one of my choosing,
> more or less

Inheritance

On my 48th birthday my mother called:
Happy Birthday. Then, *Do you have symptoms yet?*
Some gift. Some birthright. *Not yet,* I replied.
Not yet.

At fifty, my mother had signs that nothing
was as it ought to be. A grim inheritance
passed on to daughters like lace handkerchiefs
or wedding rings, but instead, shuffle-walking,

eyelids that sink to closed, and swallowing
must become an intentional act. No cure.
Oculopharyngeal Muscular Dystrophy.

The rattle of coated aspirin tablets, shaken
and taken four at a time, is iron chain links
dropping into a hollow wooden box.

The rattle of a wooden rosary gently spooled
with care into a white porcelain box is pebbles
scattering on top of a steel blue coffin.

Border Children

Choking out imprecations between angry sighs, my father,
always so good with words, can't speak. Maybe it's partly
the dentures. I don't think so. Sad and puzzled, he heaps

damnation on those who tear families apart. He misses my
mother. I do, too. No child should be separated from a parent.
I tried to protect you from your mother's anger.

Years of judgment and impossible standards destroy as much
as razor-wired walls do. Terrified children torn away from
desperate parents have slim hope of reunion without damage.

Some separations begin long before death. My mother is dead,
and we never found a safe way to cross borders. When we flee,
we save ourselves, but find separation at borders we cannot cross.

What I Would Have Kept: My Mother's Things

Not the hundreds of pairs of once-worn nylons,
not the worn-out bathrobe, piles of photos stuck
together with mildew, broken pans, the dozens
of shoes past use, the water-stained clothing,

not the stacks of monogrammed notepaper,
old pens, a basement full of damp boxes of glass
canning jars, or pilled curtains. No. None of those.

Not mismatched plates or bowls, cracked glassware,
old bath towels, not boxes of spaghetti a decade
past expiration. Not old bank books, ragged socks,
or purses full of Dentyne and tampons. None of that.

I rehomed old furniture and books and reams
and reams of colored construction paper, long
faded to a uniform beige-grey. Nothing at all.

What I would have kept wasn't there to take,
to brush and dust off, to shine and treasure.
What I would have kept was a happy memory,
a legacy that I could hold against the dark.

All I learned About Gratitude I Learned from My Mother

I learned *to mind my Ps and Qs,*
to wash my hands, and to ask please
and thank you for everything I needed.
I washed the dishes, made the meals,
baked the bread, did the laundry, hoed
and weeded and tried my best. Teen-aged
me once asked my mother why she never
said please or thank you:

I'm your mother, I don't have to.

I thank my husband.
I thank my daughter.
I thank strangers, cashiers, waitstaff,
my students, my colleagues, and friends.
Even the dog, when she gets out of my chair.

My mother never thanked me.
I learned that lesson well.

Dry Weight, Twenty-one Grams, More or Less

"MacDougall believed that the results from his experiment
showed the human soul might have weight...."

Twenty-one grams is the weight of a soul
when the fire goes out, when the juices
dry up, when the body is done extending
its reach and the fragile husk crumbles

to dust. Starfish, too, are measured in dry
weight, after the flinching body stills
and silence reigns. The shrunken disc
cannot hold the body together, cannot

sustain. Sere and curling, outstretched arms
must turn brittle in the unflinching glare
of an unshaded lamp. We are catalogued:
done from *wish*, *product* from *desire*.

Though pinned, there is no pain.
The flaking carcass remains.

Solving for X in a Pandemic

requires us to accept that x=unknown,
that x is irrational. That x cannot
be easily solved for, and x can cancel
you out. We know that x may mean ex,
as in extubation, but only if you survive.
Ex-lovers. Ex-friends. X in a pandemic
may mark the spot where you stood
when you were exposed. Extrapolate
the odds: how close were you? How long
were you nearby? Exactly who did you see
and did they test positive or negative?
Plot the X on your graph, and then
find the why.

My Father's Hands

My father's hands, once so strong,
so talented, shook. Age-spotted,
gnarled, skin paper-thin, nails broken,
jagged, thick and yellowed. His hands
coaxed music from any instrument.

Lighthouses, boats at anchor, sunsets
and darkness appeared out of pen and ink,
paper and paint. Dad wired a house, fixed
a faucet, and still had time to split and stack
firewood, brush a little girl's hair, wrap
Christmas presents, and write lyrics to songs
that will never be heard again. The last time,

Dad reached for nothing in particular,
maybe me, maybe the sheets. His hands,
bruised purple from too many IVs, were dry
and fragile like fallen leaves that skitter
across the road going nowhere in a hurry.

Breathing Exercises

Quietude is not the same thing as quiet.
       My hydrangea is white.
Disease scavenges the body, but stress
strips the soul, brings it right to the whitened
spiritual bone. Is quietus, not like death,
but calm?
       My feet rest on the floor.
A whelm of emotion hardly kept in check
brings a rictus, a ringing, a shortness
of breath.
       My dog sleeps in the sunspot on the rug.
This supercharged stillness is an ion-rich
atmosphere, a grey-green flatness preceding
strong weather. I want to be requited, acquitted,
or is that just quitting?
       My coffee is dark in my white cup.
Shoots and tubers force forth, crumble dirt,
shoulder their way upward and outward:
growth or replacement?
       I hear a lawnmower in the neighborhood.
Yellow-green paleness reminds me of death, but not
decay. Something needs light, needs air.

Free

My father departed one spring afternoon, leaving an untenanted
husk of a human home while my neighbor's trailer was gutted
by fire. I held my breath to ward off smoke and the phone call.

There's a "Free Shit" sign on my burned-out neighbor's lawn.
It's not clear if *free* is an adjective or a verb, but there's an arrow
pointing in the direction of the remains of the trailer, charred

and melted, the blackened steps leading into nowhere special.
The fire burned spectacularly, right across the street from me.
Flames guttered upward. Billows of oily, black smoke puffed

and smudged the sky at two o'clock. The street was shut down,
except for teen-agers on skateboards cluttering my driveway,
gawking in the pulsing glare of red lights probing my windows.

Does a soul burn like those wispy Pentecostal flames flickering
above each Apostle's head, wavering on the penciled page of my
catechism book? Or does it flare, then wink out? I always think
of it as a blue plume, like steam, free to leave on the last breath.

What to Keep

We hauled bags and bags and dumpster-loads
from my dad's house all last summer. There are
few objects that I prize, that I say, *That is mine!*

Things are just things. Except the little three-legged
stool. It's supposed to be a milking stool, but never
came near a cow or a goat. I sat on it, evening
after evening, while my dad dried my hair, using
the expandable hose attached to the bonnet-style
hair dryer. I can hear the hollow crinkle as it heated,

hummed, and stretched. It was a pink quilted vinyl
box like a small suitcase with a little slot through
which warm air breathed, intended for the time-

pressed housewife to dry her nails while curlers,
snug under the ballooning plastic bonnet, set her
hair into impossible sausages. But as I was saying,
before the hairdryer crept in, it was my dad who used
the wide-toothed comb and dried my hair in sections,
while I sat still in my cotton nightgown, clutching

my teddy bear, long before I loved the fur off and it lost
an eye. That stool is something I will not part with.
It is one of the few things I claimed.

That Friday

*At that moment the curtain of the temple was torn in two
from top to bottom. The earth shook, the rocks split and the
tombs broke open. —Matthew 27: 51-52*

And when the sky split, and rocks
spewed forth with the dead, did the woman
hauling water from the well push back her hair
and wonder? Or did she continue her work,

not quite sure what the omens told,
knowing only that there was dinner to get,
children to bathe, and a husband who was late
getting home from an execution across town.

Folding Laundry

I bend low to retrieve errant socks
and handkerchiefs from the still-warm
cavern of the dryer and my reaching fingers
brush against spare change, not much,

a worn dime and a few copper pennies
that shift in the drum, rattling like impatience.
It's a test: I gather fistfuls of socks
and underwear, mismatched but matched—

his and hers, ours, slightly stretched and faded.
Simple evidence of life lived in clean and quiet tandem.

Even If This is End Times, I Still

want to drink my coffee black, hot, in a pretty
mug. I want to feel sunshine on my face, stretch
out in clean, crisp sheets, and feel the heft
of a new book in my hands. I demand moments
of beauty, warm showers, fresh-baked bread,
and fuzzy slippers. I am tired of being scared,

of worrying about politicians, the climate,
the damages done, the spiteful words, the cost
of gasoline, the need to perform, the sun going
dead. I want to wake one morning, breathe deeply,
and face the day with nothing on my mind except
filling spaces between moments with flowers,
with laughter, with wonder, with you

A poet-teacher both by vocation and by trade, **Carlene M. Gadapee** is also a coffee-dependent fan of musical theatre, New England sports teams, and historical and mystery fiction. Carlene has been a public high school teacher for more than three decades, and she holds two Masters' Degrees: one in education and the other in liberal studies. Over the years, Carlene has held various positions with youth-oriented and arts non-profit organizations, most recently as associate creative director for an online series of writing seminars and workshops. Her poetry and critical reviews have appeared or are forthcoming in many publications, including *English Journal, Waterwheel Review, Gyroscope Review, Smoky Quartz, Think, Allium, Vox Populi,* and *MicroLit Almanac.* She received a "Best of the Net" nomination in 2023. Raised first in Rhode Island, and then later, in the Northeast Kingdom of Vermont, Carlene now lives in northern New Hampshire with her husband.

www.ingramcontent.com/pod-product-compliance
Lightning Source LLC
Chambersburg PA
CBHW022103080426
42734CB00009B/1476